Norwegian Word of the Day:

365 High Frequency Words to Accelerate Your Norwegian Vocabulary

Copyright © 2016

All rights reserved. No part of this publication may be reproduced, distributed, or transmitted in any form or by any means, including photocopying, recording, or other electronic or mechanical methods, without the prior written permission of the publisher.

ISBN: 1532954603
ISBN-13: 978-1532954603

CONTENTS

Introduction	i
January	1
February	9
March	16
April	24
May	32
June	40
July	48
August	56
September	64
October	72
November	80
December	88

INTRODUCTION

Learning a new language involves learning a lot of new vocabulary. Although the grammar and pronunciation of a language can seem like the most difficult parts, especially a difficult language like Norwegian, the real challenge quickly becomes learning the thousands of new words you require to speak a new language fluently.

How to find the right words and how to efficiently memorize them are the problems that many language learners face near the beginning of their studies. The goal of this book is to fill the gap by providing you with a new, high frequency Norwegian word to learn every day. At the end of the year (or much sooner) you will be 365 words closer to your goal of speaking Norwegian.

Did you know that in English, the most common 100 words make up nearly half of every sentence, and that other languages have similar frequency distributions? This is a powerful concept that is underused in many language courses. By focusing on the high frequency words, this book will accelerate your Norwegian vocabulary more efficiently than merely learning the random lists of words that learners sometimes face, and by providing the words to you, this book will save you from the time-consuming process of searching for all those new words yourself.

The outline of this book is a new word every day for a year. In this way you can be sure that you are making progress even on days where you don't have time to study. Carry this word around with you and review it throughout

INTRODUCTION

the day. Of course many people will progress faster through this book and will want more than one word a day and in that case the reader should go at whatever pace feels comfortable. I would still encourage you go back to the word of the day to review on that specific day, just to ensure that you have thoroughly learned it. Remember repetition is the mother of all learning.

Good luck on your language learning journey and I hope you enjoy your Norwegian Word of the Day!

NORWEGIAN ALPHABET AND PRONUNCIATION

The Norwegian language uses the same Latin alphabet as English, but with the addition of 3 new letters after the z. The complete Norwegian alphabet with a simple pronunciation guide for each letter is shown below:

Letter	Pronunciation
A a	"a" as in father
B b	"b" as in beer
C c	"k" as in kite before a, o, or u; "s" as in sea elsewhere
D d	"d" as in dog; after l or n or before s or t is usually silent; also often silent at the end of words
E e	"ai" as in air or "e" as in bed
F f	"f" as in feet
G g	"g" as in good normally; before i or y: "y" as in yes; silent when a word ends with ig
H h	"h" as in his; silent before a consonant
I i	"ee" as in bee or "i" as in sit
J j	"y" as in yes
K k	"k" as in kick normally; before i, j or y: a soft "sh" sound like the ch in German ich
L l	"l" as in light
M m	"m" as in meat
N n	"n" as in net

INTRODUCTION

O o	"oo" as in food or "o" as in cot
P p	"p" as in pie
Q q	similar to English (rarely used)
R r	"r" as in the Spanish toro; beginners can substitute an English "r"
S s	always "s" as in sit; never with a "z" sound like in houses
Sj sj	"sh" as in sheep
Sk sk	"sh" as in sheep
Skj skj	"sh" as in sheep
T t	"t" as in ten normally; silent when a word ends in et
U u	"u" as in butcher
V v	"v" as in van; sometimes silent at the end of words
W w	"v" as in van (rarely used)
X x	"x" as in taxi
Y y	"u" as in cute but with lips more rounded. Same as the French "u" or German "ü"
Z z	"s" as in set
Æ æ	"a" as in bad
Ø ø	"ir" as in thirst but shorter. Same as the German ö
Å å	"o" as in more or "o" as in cot

NORWEGIAN WORD OF THE DAY

Norwegian can be a difficult language to pronounce. In addition to some difficult sounds, many Norwegian words have silent letters and it is not always clear from the written word how it should be pronounced. If you are unsure about the pronunciation, I recommend going to forvo.com and typing in the Norwegian word to hear a native speaker pronounce it.

There are three noun genders in Norwegian, masculine, feminine and neuter. The gender of the noun is important to know, as the noun and adjective forms are affected by the noun's gender. The gender is given below each noun in this book so that it can be learned along with the word on that day.

NORWEGIAN WORD OF THE DAY

Jan. 1

by

city (masculine)

Jan. 2

synge

to sing

Jan. 3

ild

fire (masculine)

Jan. 4

landsby

village (masculine)

JANUARY

Jan. 5

bar

bar (place to drink) (masculine)

Jan. 6

kone

wife (feminine)

Jan. 7

middag

dinner (masculine)

Jan. 8

pepper

pepper (neuter)

NORWEGIAN WORD OF THE DAY

Jan. 9

land

country (neuter)

Jan. 10

stor

big

Jan. 11

vest

west (neuter)

Jan. 12

vår

spring (masculine)

JANUARY

Jan. 13

flyge

to fly

Jan. 14

seng

bed (masculine)

Jan. 15

lese

to read

Jan. 16

kart

map (neuter)

Jan. 17

blomst

flower (masculine)

Jan. 18

hav

sea (neuter)

Jan. 19

klokke

clock (feminine)

Jan. 20

sekund

second (neuter)

JANUARY

Jan. 21

tørr

dry

Jan. 22

vindu

window (neuter)

Jan. 23

stasjon

train station (masculine)

Jan. 24

svart

black

Jan. 25

fugl

bird (masculine)

Jan. 26

lufthavn

airport (feminine)

Jan. 27

kultur

culture (masculine)

Jan. 28

hatt

hat (masculine)

JANUARY

Jan. 29

ond

evil

Jan. 30

sol

sun (feminine)

Jan. 31

stjerne

star (feminine)

NORWEGIAN WORD OF THE DAY

Feb. 1

kake

cake (masculine)

Feb. 2

kaffe

coffee (masculine)

Feb. 3

historie

story (masculine)

Feb. 4

viktig

important

FEBRUARY

Feb. 5

møte

meeting (neuter)

Feb. 6

svette

sweat (feminine)

Feb. 7

tog

train (neuter)

Feb. 8

skole

school (masculine)

Feb. 9

tre

tree (neuter)

Feb. 10

ansikt

face (neuter)

Feb. 11

venn

friend (masculine)

Feb. 12

hvordan

how

Feb. 13

ku

cow (feminine)

Feb. 14

bedstefar

grandfather (masculine)

Feb. 15

te

tea (masculine)

Feb. 16

oransje

orange (color)

Feb. 17

natt

night (masculine)

Feb. 18

butikk

store / shop (masculine)

Feb. 19

ren

clean

Feb. 20

ny

new

FEBRUARY

Feb. 21

rik

rich

Feb. 22

alltid

always

Feb. 23

se

to see

Feb. 24

penn

pen (masculine)

NORWEGIAN WORD OF THE DAY

Feb. 25

park

park (masculine)

Feb. 26

svømme

to swim

Feb. 27

datter

daughter (feminine)

Feb. 28

skubbe

to push

MARCH

Mar. 1

skog

forest (masculine)

Mar. 2

blyant

pencil (masculine)

Mar. 3

død

dead

Mar. 4

språk

language (neuter)

Mar. 5

gris

pig (masculine)

Mar. 6

måned

month (masculine)

Mar. 7

kniv

knife (masculine)

Mar. 8

øst

east (neuter)

MARCH

Mar. 9

lukke

to close

Mar. 10

hus

house (neuter)

Mar. 11

våkne

to wake up

Mar. 12

kald

cold

Mar. 13

ben

leg (neuter)

Mar. 14

flod

river (masculine)

Mar. 15

soldat

soldier (masculine)

Mar. 16

gress

grass (neuter)

Mar. 17

gulv

floor (neuter)

Mar. 18

blod

blood (neuter)

Mar. 19

sove

to sleep

Mar. 20

snø

snow (masculine)

Mar. 21

sønn

son (masculine)

Mar. 22

eple

apple (neuter)

Mar. 23

varm

hot

Mar. 24

morgen

morning (masculine)

Mar. 25

søle

mud (feminine)

Mar. 26

bord

table (neuter)

Mar. 27

tunge

tongue (feminine)

Mar. 28

far

father (masculine)

Mar. 29

storfekjøtt

beef (neuter)

Mar. 30

tå

toe (feminine)

Mar. 31

pil

arrow (feminine)

APRIL

Apr. 1

olje

oil (cooking) (feminine)

Apr. 2

menneske

human (neuter)

Apr. 3

vaske

to wash

Apr. 4

klær

clothing (plural)

Apr. 5

frakk

coat (masculine)

Apr. 6

regn

rain (neuter)

Apr. 7

når

when

Apr. 8

følge

to follow

APRIL

Apr. 9

papir

paper (neuter)

Apr. 10

lett

easy

Apr. 11

hode

head (neuter)

Apr. 12

bestemor

grandmother (feminine)

Apr. 13

appelsin

orange (fruit) (masculine)

Apr. 14

kaste

to throw

Apr. 15

rygg

back (body) (masculine)

Apr. 16

dag

day (masculine)

Apr. 17

nord

north (neuter)

Apr. 18

hjerte

heart (neuter)

Apr. 19

begynne

to begin

Apr. 20

hund

dog (masculine)

Apr. 21

grønn

green

Apr. 22

ordbok

dictionary (feminine)

Apr. 23

leppe

lip (feminine)

Apr. 24

kirsebær

cherry (neuter)

Apr. 25

lunsj

lunch (masculine)

Apr. 26

høst

autumn (masculine)

Apr. 27

idé

idea (masculine)

Apr. 28

skjegg

beard (neuter)

NORWEGIAN WORD OF THE DAY

Apr. 29

glad

happy

Apr. 30

elske

to love

May 1

luft

air (masculine)

May 2

i går

yesterday

May 3

brød

bread (neuter)

May 4

veske

bag (feminine)

May 5

hjul

wheel (neuter)

May 6

ville

to want

May 7

tann

tooth (feminine)

May 8

glemme

to forget

May 9

våpen

weapon (neuter)

May 10

lukte

to smell

May 11

navn

name (neuter)

May 12

løpe

to run

May 13

dyr

animal (neuter)

May 14

halvdel

half (masculine)

May 15

stol

chair (masculine)

May 16

drepe

to kill

May 17

gråte

to cry

May 18

noen

somebody

May 19

snakke

to speak

May 20

gård

farm (masculine)

May 21

danse

to dance

May 22

selge

to sell

May 23

rød

red

May 24

salat

salad (masculine)

May 25

bil

car (masculine)

May 26

gulrot

carrot (feminine)

May 27

sommer

summer (masculine)

May 28

kylling

chicken (masculine)

May 29

salt

salt (neuter)

May 30

lytte

to listen

May 31

vitenskap

science (masculine)

JUNE

Jun. 1

år

year (neuter)

Jun. 2

jente

girl (feminine)

Jun. 3

skjære

to cut

Jun. 4

mange

many

Jun. 5

lege

doctor (masculine)

Jun. 6

problem

problem (neuter)

Jun. 7

støvel

boot (masculine)

Jun. 8

bjørn

bear (masculine)

Jun. 9

vin

wine (masculine)

Jun. 10

finne

to find

Jun. 11

hud

skin (masculine)

Jun. 12

bror

brother (masculine)

Jun. 13

parkere

to park

Jun. 14

kysse

to kiss

Jun. 15

verden

world (masculine)

Jun. 16

tykk

thick

Jun. 17

noe

something

Jun. 18

vind

wind (masculine)

Jun. 19

forskjellig

different

Jun. 20

fly

airplane (neuter)

NORWEGIAN WORD OF THE DAY

Jun. 21

svinekjøtt

pork (neuter)

Jun. 22

katt

cat (masculine)

Jun. 23

samme

same

Jun. 24

slåss

to fight

Jun. 25

kjøkken

kitchen (neuter)

Jun. 26

sykkel

bicycle (masculine)

Jun. 27

skje

spoon (masculine)

Jun. 28

sykehus

hospital (neuter)

Jun. 29

banan

banana (masculine)

Jun. 30

lommebok

wallet (masculine)

JULY

Jul. 1

hva

what

Jul. 2

grønnsak

vegetable (feminine)

Jul. 3

ulv

wolf (masculine)

Jul. 4

frokost

breakfast (masculine)

Jul. 5

hvit

white

Jul. 6

bryllup

wedding (neuter)

Jul. 7

mus

mouse (feminine)

Jul. 8

dyrt

expensive

Jul. 9

arbeide

to work

Jul. 10

hvor

where

Jul. 11

kirke

church (feminine)

Jul. 12

stå

to stand

Jul. 13

kanskje

maybe

Jul. 14

kamera

camera (neuter)

Jul. 15

blå

blue

Jul. 16

tomat

tomato (masculine)

Jul. 17

advokat

lawyer (masculine)

Jul. 18

tynn

thin

Jul. 19

nøkkel

key (masculine)

Jul. 20

gutt

boy (masculine)

Jul. 21

ost

cheese (masculine)

Jul. 22

tidlig

early

Jul. 23

suppe

soup (feminine)

Jul. 24

rom

room (neuter)

Jul. 25

billett

ticket (masculine)

Jul. 26

spise

to eat

Jul. 27

fjernsyn

television (neuter)

Jul. 28

bygge

to build

Jul. 29

juice

juice (masculine)

Jul. 30

nå

now

Jul. 31

øye

eye (neuter)

AUGUST

Aug. 1

sokk

sock (masculine)

Aug. 2

avis

newspaper (feminine)

Aug. 3

nese

nose (feminine)

Aug. 4

lage mat

to cook

Aug. 5

toalett

bathroom / toilet (neuter)

Aug. 6

kjøpe

to buy

Aug. 7

mor

mother (feminine)

Aug. 8

le

to laugh

AUGUST

Aug. 9

fange

to catch

Aug. 10

paraply

umbrella (masculine)

Aug. 11

åpne

to open

Aug. 12

drue

grape (feminine)

Aug. 13

stemme

voice (masculine)

Aug. 14

himmel

sky (masculine)

Aug. 15

medisin

medicine (masculine)

Aug. 16

skrive

to write

Aug. 17

tastatur

keyboard (neuter)

Aug. 18

lærer

teacher (masculine)

Aug. 19

kunst

art (feminine)

Aug. 20

høy

tall

Aug. 21

håpe

to hope

Aug. 22

øy

island (feminine)

Aug. 23

frukt

fruit (feminine)

Aug. 24

tro

to believe

AUGUST

Aug. 25

minutt

minute (neuter)

Aug. 26

gjerde

fence (neuter)

Aug. 27

betale

to pay

Aug. 28

sko

shoe (masculine)

Aug. 29

syk

sick

Aug. 30

lys

light (neuter)

Aug. 31

søster

sister (feminine)

Sep. 1

bok

book (feminine)

Sep. 2

vinter

winter (masculine)

Sep. 3

billig

cheap

Sep. 4

stille

quiet

Sep. 5

øre

ear (neuter)

Sep. 6

bukse

pants (feminine)

Sep. 7

kvinne

woman (feminine)

Sep. 8

vanskelig

difficult

SEPTEMBER

Sep. 9

leke

to play

Sep. 10

sitte

to sit

Sep. 11

soveværelse

bedroom (neuter)

Sep. 12

dør

door (masculine)

Sep. 13

spill

game (neuter)

Sep. 14

falle

to fall

Sep. 15

sein

late

Sep. 16

drøm

dream (masculine)

Sep. 17

finger

finger (masculine)

Sep. 18

penger

money (plural)

Sep. 19

i live

alive

Sep. 20

trekke

to pull

Sep. 21

vokse

to grow

Sep. 22

uke

week (feminine)

Sep. 23

vann

water (neuter)

Sep. 24

hvem

who

Sep. 25

liten

small

Sep. 26

vinne

to win

Sep. 27

lage

to make

Sep. 28

smal

narrow

Sep. 29

trist

sad

Sep. 30

vakker

beautiful

OCTOBER

Oct. 1

gate

street (feminine)

Oct. 2

svak

weak

Oct. 3

fisk

fish (masculine)

Oct. 4

hoppe

to jump

Oct. 5

langsom

slow

Oct. 6

månen

moon (masculine)

Oct. 7

egg

egg (neuter)

Oct. 8

tau

rope (neuter)

Oct. 9

våt

wet

Oct. 10

kopp

cup (masculine)

Oct. 11

time

hour (masculine)

Oct. 12

lam

lamb (neuter)

Oct. 13

tape

to lose

Oct. 14

fattig

poor

Oct. 15

potet

potato (masculine)

Oct. 16

framtid

future (feminine)

OCTOBER

Oct. 17

buss

bus (masculine)

Oct. 18

sør

south (neuter)

Oct. 19

museum

museum (neuter)

Oct. 20

lære

to learn

Oct. 21

arm

arm (masculine)

Oct. 22

klatre

to climb

Oct. 23

is

ice (masculine)

Oct. 24

skinke

ham (feminine)

Oct. 25

hage

garden (masculine)

Oct. 26

sport

sport (masculine)

Oct. 27

kontor

office (neuter)

Oct. 28

dø

to die

Oct. 29

huske

to remember

Oct. 30

hår

hair (neuter)

Oct. 31

sterk

strong

NOVEMBER

Nov. 1

rask

fast

Nov. 2

familie

family (masculine)

Nov. 3

blad

leaf (neuter)

Nov. 4

i dag

today

Nov. 5

fred

peace (masculine)

Nov. 6

ingenting

nothing

Nov. 7

innsjø

lake (masculine)

Nov. 8

øl

beer (masculine)

Nov. 9

mann

man (masculine)

Nov. 10

flaske

bottle (feminine)

Nov. 11

i morgen

tomorrow

Nov. 12

lang

long

Nov. 13

lyve

to tell a lie

Nov. 14

hotell

hotel (neuter)

Nov. 15

vegetarianer

vegetarian (masculine)

Nov. 16

politi

police (neuter)

NOVEMBER

Nov. 17

interessant

interesting

Nov. 18

slå

to hit

Nov. 19

fjell

mountain (neuter)

Nov. 20

metall

metal (neuter)

Nov. 21

vegg

wall (masculine)

Nov. 22

høyre

right

Nov. 23

skål

bowl (feminine)

Nov. 24

gul

yellow

Nov. 25

hals

neck (masculine)

Nov. 26

batteri

battery (neuter)

Nov. 27

musikk

music (masculine)

Nov. 28

gå

to walk

Nov. 29

kjøre

to drive

Nov. 30

tak

roof (neuter)

DECEMBER

Dec. 1

venstre

left

Dec. 2

kropp

body (masculine)

Dec. 3

skitten

dirty

Dec. 4

ingen

nobody

Dec. 5

stygg

ugly

Dec. 6

båt

boat (masculine)

Dec. 7

allerede

already

Dec. 8

krig

war (masculine)

Dec. 9

tallerken

plate (masculine)

Dec. 10

vid

wide

Dec. 11

smør

butter (neuter)

Dec. 12

kjole

dress (masculine)

Dec. 13

hjerne

brain (masculine)

Dec. 14

gaffel

fork (masculine)

Dec. 15

drikke

to drink

Dec. 16

vite

to know

Dec. 17

litt

a little

Dec. 18

hjelpe

to help

Dec. 19

student

student (masculine)

Dec. 20

sten

stone (masculine)

Dec. 21

datamaskin

computer (masculine)

Dec. 22

bro

bridge (feminine)

Dec. 23

smile

to smile

Dec. 24

kjedelig

boring

Dec. 25

melk

milk (masculine)

Dec. 26

hest

horse (masculine)

Dec. 27

skjørt

skirt (neuter)

Dec. 28

restaurant

restaurant (masculine)

Dec. 29

kort

short

Dec. 30

munn

mouth (masculine)

Dec. 31

lomme

pocket (feminine)

Made in the USA
Middletown, DE
28 November 2017